Classic Recipes of
RUSSIA

Classic Recipes of RUSSIA

TRADITIONAL FOOD AND COOKING
IN 25 AUTHENTIC DISHES

ELENA MAKHONKO

LORENZ BOOKS

This edition is published by
Lorenz Books
an imprint of Anness Publishing Ltd
info@anness.com
www.lorenzbooks.com
www.annesspublishing.com

If you like the images in this book and
would like to investigate using them for
publishing, promotions or advertising,
please visit our website
www.practicalpictures.com for more
information.

Publisher: Joanna Lorenz
Editor: Emma Clegg & Helen Sudell
Designer: Nigel Partridge
Production Controller: Ben Worley
Recipe Photography: Martin Brigdale

The image on the front cover is of Small
Blueberry Pies, page 56

A CIP catalogue record for this book is
available from the British Library

PUBLISHER'S NOTE

Although the advice and information in this
book are believed to be accurate and true
at the time of going to press, neither the
author nor the publisher can accept any
legal responsibility or liability for any errors
or omissions that may have been made nor
for any inaccuracies nor for any loss, harm
or injury that comes about from following
instructions or advice in this book.

PUBLISHER'S ACKNOWLEDGMENTS

The Publisher would like to thank
iStockphoto: p6, p8 bl, tc, p10 bl, p11 bl, tr
for the use of their images.

COOK'S NOTES

Bracketed terms are intended for American
readers. For all recipes, quantities are given
in both metric and imperial measures and,
where appropriate, in standard cups and
spoons. Follow one set of measures, but
not a mixture, because they are not
interchangeable.

Standard spoon and cup measures are
level. 1 tsp = 5ml, 1 tbsp = 15ml, 1 cup =
250ml/8fl oz. Australian standard
tablespoons are 20ml. Australian readers
should use 3 tsp in place of 1 tbsp for
measuring small quantities.

American pints are 16fl oz/2 cups.
American readers should use 20fl oz/2.5
cups in place of 1 pint when measuring
liquids.

Electric oven temperatures in this book are
for conventional ovens. When using a fan
oven, the temperature will probably need to
be reduced by about 10–20°C/20–40°F.
Since ovens vary, you should check with
your manufacturer's instruction book for
guidance.

The nutritional analysis given for each
recipe is calculated per portion (i.e. serving
or item), unless otherwise stated. If the
recipe gives a range, such as Serves 4–6,
then the nutritional analysis will be for the
smaller portion size, i.e. 6 servings. The
analysis does not include optional
ingredients, such as salt added to taste.

Medium (US large) eggs are used unless
otherwise stated.

Contents

Introduction

Russian recipes are passed through the generations and cooking is taught from a young age. Most families follow their *babushka's* (grandmother's) advice and in this way each family has developed their own versions of traditional Russian recipes. As most of Russia is located north of the 51st latitude Russians are used to the cold, and also to the scarcity of food during the winter months, and have developed all sorts of recipes for making filling dishes out of a few locally available ingredients. During the summer, Russia's extensive coastline offers much in the way of fresh fish and the warmer southern regions provide much-needed wheat, vegetables, herbs, fruits, honey, wine and yogurt.

Left: Traditional farming methods are still employed throughout Russia as these beautiful haystacks testify in the fertile Caucasus region.

Russian Food Culture

The company of family and friends is just as important as the meal itself to most Russians, and they like nothing better than planning the recipes, shopping for the right ingredients, eating the food and discussing it afterwards. Although Russians today shop at supermarkets, where they can buy typical Russian fare as well as imported delicacies, there are also special food market stalls entirely devoted to either pickled

Below: Russians love pancakes, whether dripping with honey or packed full of fresh fruits.

Above: Fried dumplings are added to many hearty stews and casseroles.

vegetables or many kinds of dried fruit. Fresh bread is usually bought from the baker.

The typical Russian way of cooking is to make large batches of food at one time. Casseroles and soups are made in large 7-litre pans and nobody thinks twice about eating the same food for as much as four days in a row.

Breakfast is usually a cup of tea with sugar and a slice of lemon, and maybe a piece of bread or cake to go with it.

The classical Russian lunch is often taken in a stolovaja.

These are simple cafeterias where students and employees eat an inexpensive lunch of genuine Russian food. Usually there are three courses to choose from, including a soup. As always in Russia bread and tea is served with the food.

Dinner is the main meal of the day. In past times, when many people were working hard on the land, it would be a substantial affair to keep up the energy levels. The nobility stretched this meal into several courses, while peasants might be on basic rations of bread and soup, maybe with a little meat or fish. These days, if it is a special occasion there will be some appetizers (zakuski), a thick, rich soup, a variety of small courses served together, or a main course of meat, fish or poultry. Desserts are usually light and based on fruit after the previous rich and substantial savoury courses.

Right: Wholesome, protein-rich soups play an important role in Russian culinary culture.

Traditional Russian Dishes

The basic foods eaten every day in Russia are quite simple. The particular flavour of Russian cuisine lies in the way the ingredients are combined, and the typical seasonings used.

Pelmenis

These little pasta rolls (also known as peljmenis), filled with meat, are something between dim sum and ravioli. They are usually home-made in large batches. One person takes care of the dough, another mixes the meat, and a third fills the little rolls with the filling. When it is time to eat, the pelmeni are

Below: Frozen pelmeni ready to be cooked to order.

boiled from frozen and served with sour cream, a drop of vinegar and salt and freshly ground pepper. Forty pelmeni per person is a normal portion.

Pastries

Savoury pastries are a meal in themselves, filled with meat, vegetables, or mushrooms. Sweet pastries contain fruit or berries and cottage cheese, and are a favourite snack to be taken with tea. There are all sorts of different specialities such as pirogi, kulebjaka and rastegaj, all made with the same kind of dough.

Blinis

Outside Russia blinis are small, thick buckwheat pancakes, but Russians make their blinis with wheat flour. They are often as large and thin as the most delicate crêpes. For Russians, blinis symbolize life and fertility. During Maslenitsa, a festival to celebrate the return of spring, blinis are the main food for a week. They are also eaten to excess before the start of Lent.

Above: Little potato pies make a filling lunch.

Soup

No other cuisine can present such a wide variety of soups as the Russian tradition. Russian soups are often thick and rich and every home has its own secret recipes passed down from older generations. In Russia, soup is either served as the first course, or between the appetizer and the main course. Borscht, its most famous soup, is said to come from Ukraine, but nobody is sure of its true origin. There are many recipes for borscht but all of course feature beetroot (beet), which gives it its ruby red colour.

Meat and Fish

Russians are a meat-loving people and eat meat almost every day if they are not on a religious fast. Jorkoje, bite-sized pieces of meat fried on the stove, is popular. Another favourite is sashlik, a kebab of barbecued meat, usually lamb or pork.

With so many natural fishing waters, fish is bound to appear on the Russian dinner table. It is normally cooked at its freshest, coated in breadcrumbs and lightly fried.

Below: Tea would be served from the samovar with zakuski.

Above: Barbecued kebabs are a popular summer treat.

Zakuski

These famous appetizers are an old Russian tradition that first appeared in Russian manor houses. Guests arriving after a long journey would be greeted with a table of zakuski in the hallway. On the table, the carafe containing vodka was given the place of honour and during the winter the samovar was constantly sizzling with hot tea. The zakuski table mirrored the hospitality that Russians are so famous for.

Any time is the right time to serve zakuski. They are perfect to serve as an appetizer or as a main course. The meal starts with the host offering a toast – 'za zdorovie!' (good health). The first dish is a simple plate of salted cucumber in sour cream and honey. Next, a fish dish of herring and caviar with newly boiled potatoes. Then comes the meat and vegetables and an array of different pickles. All of this is washed down with ice cold vodka or Russian champagne.

Classic Ingredients

Russia is like a giant pantry, full of all that the good earth yields from rivers and lakes, forests and meadows. The woods are full of seasonal harvests of berries, mushrooms and herbs. The rivers and lakes teem with freshwater fish like carp, bream and pike while the green pastures support both meat and milk production. Russians are proud of their fertile land and are expert at growing the staple ingredients themselves.

Grains

No Russian meal would be complete without rye or wheat bread. The meal is simply not

Below: Buckwheat is used to add substance to casseroles.

ready to serve until the bread is put out. Other grains such as pearl barley, buckwheat and rice are also popular, and add substance to soups and stews.

Vegetables

The fertility of the soil and the culture of maintaining a kitchen garden have led to an emphasis on vegetables of all kinds in Russian cuisine.

Cabbage is a real staple food in Russia with the large outer leaves used for cabbage rolls stuffed with meat or fish. The inner leaves are used in soups and raw salads. Preserved cabbage, sauerkraut, plays an important role in Russian cuisine.

The immensely popular beetroot (beet) are not only used in borscht soup, they are used in many salads, and form the basis of a topping for blinis known as beetroot caviar.

Potatoes are ubiquitous in Russian cooking, whether as a separate accompaniment, in a stew, or cooked and cooled as part of a salad. Cold boiled potatoes with a sour cream

Above: Wild mushrooms are still foraged in Russian forests.

dressing and plenty of dill are a favourite part of the zakuski table. Other vegetables used are swede, black radish, carrots, onions and turnips

Earthy rich mushrooms are an integral part of many Russian recipes – in soups, appetizers, sauces and in fillings for pies and pastries,

Salted cucumber, made by preserving them with herbs or garlic, are eaten with sour cream as zakuski, added to soups and made into sauces.

Right: Root vegetables, such as beetroot (beet) are loved by Russian cooks.

Above: Smetana is used as a topping and as a thickener.

Dairy produce

Cow's milk is not much used in Russia, but other products from the dairy are popular, such as yogurt, cottage cheese and curd (farmer's) cheese. Smetana, a sharp, thick sour cream is an important ingredient, frequently added as a thickener in soups and sauces and as a topping for all kinds of foods.

Eggs

Chicken eggs were very precious to the peasant population and they are as indispensable today, being used in pelmeni (pasta dumplings), lapsha, sweet cakes, omelettes and pancakes.

Meat, poultry and game

Russians love meat and it often forms the main course for lunch or supper and always for larger celebratory meals. On these occasions the meat is often prepared whole, and roasted suckling pig, chicken or goose are characteristic dishes for Easter or New Year feasts. One of the most well-known Russian dishes is Beef Stroganoff, a rich mixture of best-quality beef with sour cream.

Below: Cod steak is delicious lightly fried in oil.

Above: Pancakes and blinis are popular dishes made with eggs.

Chicken and goose dishes feature often on the Russian table and the famous Chicken Kiev from Ukraine has been adopted by cooks throughout the world.

Animals such as rabbit, deer and hare are still hunted in the forests of rural Russia. These strong-tasting game meats are either slow-cooked in the oven or simmered in a sauce to tenderize them.

Fish

Russian cuisine offers a wide variety of both cold and hot fish dishes. Large white sea fish such as flounder, sole or halibut

Above: Fresh parsley adds distinctive flavour to many dishes.

can be baked whole in the oven, or chopped into pieces to be simmered in a sauce. The huge lakes and rivers of Russia provide many varieties of fish and there are many recipes that

Below: Aromatic poppy seeds are added to cakes and breads.

feature pike, perch, and carp. The roe from cod or pike used to be the single most important dish on the table, but over time sturgeon caviar has become the most popular.

Spices and flavourings

Russian dishes are enlivened by a whole range of herbs, spices and flavourings grown in rural Russia. Dill and parsley are the most commonly used herbs, blending well with many vegetables, particularly potato. Russian cuisine is generally quite mild but can be given a little extra zing in the form of shredded fresh horseradish. In common with most Eastern countries, fragrant poppy seeds are a favourite in Russia, often used as a topping to be sprinkled over sweet dishes. Garlic is used to add its own distinctive aromatic flavour.

Berries

Russians are very diligent at finding and preserving what nature provides, and berry picking with the family is one of

Above: Garlic is used often in Caucasian cooking.

their great pleasures. Russians love the sour taste of cranberries, which are used to make the drink mors. Other berries are used in cakes and desserts and for making jam and preserves.

Below: Cranberries are used in many tempting desserts.

With Love from Russia

Mention Russian food, and most people will conjure up an image of a tureen of ruby-red borscht, warm blinis with melted butter, exclusive caviar from the Caspian Sea and maybe Beef Stroganoff or Chicken Kiev. But there is more – much more. A country as enormous as Russia, with so many variations in climate, geography and culture, has a lot to offer anybody interested in wholesome good food. Russians have also always loved to party, and enjoying good food and drink with family and friends is the true Russian way of life.

Left: Pelmenis have a spicy meat filling and are a traditional snack throughout Russia.

Beetroot Soup Borscht

Serves 4–6

5–6 beetroots (beets), total weight
    500g/1¼lb
3 carrots, total weight 250g/9oz
1 cabbage wedge, total weight
    300g/11oz
2 onions
3 potatoes
45ml/3 tbsp tomato purée (paste)
15ml/1 tbsp sugar
5ml/1 tsp salt
60–90ml/4–6 tbsp smetana or
    crème fraîche
chopped fresh dill, to garnish
4–6 lemon wedges, to serve

For the stock

1kg/2¼lb beef on the bone
2 litres/3½ pints/8 cups water
1 carrot
1 parsnip
1 piece celeriac
1 onion
2 bay leaves
4–5 black peppercorns
2–3 fresh parsley stalks
5ml/1 tsp salt

1 To make the stock, put the beef and bones in a large pan, add the water and bring to the boil. Lower the heat and simmer for 10 minutes, skimming the surface of any residue that rises to the top.

2 Add the carrot, parsnip, celeriac, onion, bay leaves, peppercorns, parsley and salt to the pan. Cover and simmer gently for approximately 1 hour. Remove the vegetables and seasonings from the pan and discard them. Remove the meat from the pan and cut into small chunks.

3 To make the soup, add the beetroots and carrots to the pan, bring to the boil then simmer for about 40 minutes, until the vegetables are tender. Remove the beetroots and carrots from the pan and leave to cool.

4 Meanwhile, slice the cabbage and onions and dice the potatoes. Add to the pan, bring the stock back to the boil then simmer for 20 minutes.

5 Coarsely grate the cooled beetroots and carrots. When the cabbage, onions and potatoes are tender, add the beetroot and carrot to the soup with the tomato purée, sugar and salt. Add the meat. Simmer for a further 10 minutes.

6 To serve, pour the soup into warmed bowls. Top each serving with 2–3 pieces of meat, 15ml/1 tbsp smetana or crème fraîche and chopped dill to garnish. Accompany with a lemon wedge.

This famous soup is the centre and highlight of the Russian meal. There are many versions of the recipe, which are often passed on in the family, and the young are taught to cook it from a very early age. The secret behind a good borscht is the home-made stock and the high quality of the root vegetables used.

Fresh Cabbage Soup
Svegii Stjii

1 Melt the butter in a large pan over a medium heat. Add the onion and cook, stirring frequently, for 3 minutes, until softened but not browned. Add the cabbage, carrot and celeriac and cook for 3 minutes.

2 Add the bay leaves, peppercorns and 200ml/7fl oz/scant 1 cup of stock. Bring to the boil then reduce the heat, cover and simmer for 15 minutes, stirring occasionally.

3 Add the remaining stock and the potatoes and simmer for a further 10 minutes until the potatoes are soft.

4 Meanwhile, heat the oil in a small frying pan over medium heat. Add the pepper and tomatoes and fry for 2–3 minutes, until softened.

5 Transfer the pepper and tomatoes to the soup and simmer for 5 minutes. Season with salt and pepper to taste.

6 Spoon the soup into bowls, and sprinkle with the chopped dill. Top with smetana or crème fraîche and accompany with rye bread.

Serves 4

40g/1½oz/3 tbsp butter
1 onion, sliced
1 head white cabbage, total weight
 750g/1lb 10oz, shredded
1 carrot, shredded or grated
1 piece celeriac, total weight
 50g/2oz, shredded and grated
2 bay leaves
5 black peppercorns
1.5 litres/2½ pints/6¼ cups
 vegetable stock
5 new potatoes, diced
15ml/1 tbsp sunflower oil
1 (bell) pepper, cored and sliced
2 tomatoes, chopped
salt and ground black pepper
45ml/3 tbsp chopped fresh dill, to
 garnish
smetana or crème fraîche and rye
 bread, to serve

Soups play an important part in Russian cuisine and this vegetarian soup is one of the most popular everyday soups. Every housewife has her own recipe and the variations and adaptations are endless.

Cold Kvass Soup Okroshka

1 Put the eggs in a pan, cover with cold water and bring to the boil. Reduce the heat and simmer for 10 minutes. Drain and put under cold running water. Shell the eggs and separate the yolks from the whites.

2 Put the egg yolks in a soup tureen or bowl and mash until smooth. Add the mustard and the smetana or crème fraîche and mix together. Slowly mix in the kvass or buttermilk.

3 Chop the egg whites. Dice the meat or sausages. Finely slice the cucumber and spring onions. Add the meat, cucumber, spring onions, and egg whites to the egg yolk mixture and mix together. Add the sugar and dill and season with salt to taste.

4 To serve, pour the soup into soup bowls and top with the remaining smetana or crème fraîche.

COOK'S TIP
If you cannot find kvass, a sweet, wheat- based drink, buttermilk will give a different but equally good flavour.

Serves 4
2 eggs
15ml/1 tbsp mustard
100ml/3½fl oz/scant ½ cup
    smetana or crème fraîche plus
    60ml/4 tbsp, to serve
1 litre/1¾ pints/4 cups kvass or
    buttermilk (see Cook's tip)
250g/9oz cooked meat, such as
    unsmoked ham or roast pork, or
    cooked sausages
1 cucumber, total weight 250g/9oz
1 bunch spring onions (scallions)
15ml/1 tbsp sugar
45ml/3 tbsp finely chopped fresh dill
salt

Kvass is a fermented drink, low in alcohol, which is made from wheat. It can also be used as a basis for this soup, known as okroshka. This soup is very easy to make and is perfect on a lazy summer day. Chilled, tasty okroshka will cool you when the temperature rises.

Makes 20

25g/1oz fresh yeast
5ml/1 tsp caster (superfine) sugar
50ml/2fl oz/¼ cup warm (37°C/98°F)
　water
2 egg yolks
250ml/8fl oz/1 cup warm
　(37°C/98°F) milk
2.5ml/½ tsp salt
175g/6oz/1½ cups plain white
　(all-purpose) flour
3 egg whites
150ml/¼ pint/⅔ cup rapeseed
　(canola) oil

For the toppings

slices of smoked salmon
pickled herring, chopped
chopped onion
smetana or crème fraîche
caviar
lemon wedges and dill, to garnish

Russian Pancakes Blini

1 Put the yeast, sugar and warm water in a small bowl and blend until smooth. Leave in a warm place for 20 minutes until frothy.

2 Mix together the egg yolks, 200ml/6fl oz/¾ cup of the warm milk and the salt in a large bowl. Stir in the yeast mixture and the flour, a little at a time, to form a smooth batter. Leave the batter to rise in a warm place for 4–5 hours, stirring three or four times during that time.

3 Stir the remainder 50ml/2fl oz/¼ cup of the milk into the batter. Whisk the egg whites in a dry bowl until they form soft peaks.

4 Fold the egg whites into the batter and set aside for 30 minutes.

5 Heat the oil in a frying pan and add 25–30ml/1½–2 tbsp of batter for each blini. Fry gently over a medium heat until the batter has set and risen. Turn the blinis over and cook the second side. Continue to cook the remaining batter to make 20 blinis.

6 Your guests can choose their own toppings or you can assemble the blinis yourself. Never use onion with caviar, and if you have real Russian black caviar serve it on its own on the blini, with a spoonful of smetana or crème fraîche on the side.

COOK'S TIP

Make the batter for the blinis at least 3 hours before frying, as this allows the yeast to rise fully. Stir the batter 3–4 times while rising.

These little pancakes are delicious served with caviar or smoked salmon, or with smetana, soused herring and chopped onion. Blinis can be served with a topping, or served separately so people can make their own.

Salted Cucumbers Smedomi

Makes 1kg/2¼lb

1kg/2¼lb mini cucumbers or
   medium, fresh gherkins, or regular
   cucumbers
10 blackcurrant leaves
10 garlic cloves
3–4 dill sprigs with flowers
1–2 bay leaves
50g/2oz fresh horseradish, finely
   diced
20 black peppercorns

For the marinade

1 litre/1¾ pints/4 cups water
2.5ml/½ tsp red or white wine
   vinegar
45ml/3 tbsp salt

To serve 2 as an appetizer

5ml/1 tsp lemon juice
60ml/4 tbsp smetana or crème
   fraîche
60ml/4 tbsp clear honey
Russian vodka

*Salted cucumbers are the
most popular zakuski dish
and a cherished ingredient
in Russian cooking. Serve
with Russian vodka.*

1 To prepare the marinade for the cucumbers, put all the ingredients in a pan, bring to the boil then remove from the heat and leave to cool.

2 If you can find mini cucumbers or fresh gherkins, prick all over with a fork; if you are using a large cucumber, cut it into thick fingers.

3 Put the cucumbers into one or several clean, dry glass jars, layering them with blackcurrant leaves, garlic cloves, dill sprigs, bay leaves, horseradish and peppercorns.

4 Pour in the marinade to cover, and seal the jars. Leave to marinate for 5–6 hours. Then store the jars in the refrigerator for at least 2–3 weeks.

5 To serve, place the cucumbers in a serving bowl, cutting into fingers if they were salted whole. Mix the lemon juice with the smetana or crème fraîche. Put the honey in a separate small serving bowl. To eat, dip the cucumbers in honey or smetana or crème fraîche. Serve with vodka.

Beetroot Caviar Ikra iz Svekly

Serves 4–8
1 onion, total weight 150g/5oz
4 medium cooked beetroots (beets)
45ml/3 tbsp rapeseed (canola) oil
30ml/2 tbsp tomato purée (paste)
salt and ground black pepper
12 small pieces rye bread, to serve
finely chopped fresh parsley, to
    garnish

1 Chop the onion and coarsely grate the beetroots. Heat the oil in a medium pan, add the onion and fry gently for 5–8 minutes, until softened and golden brown.

2 Add the grated beetroot to the onion and fry, stirring all the time, for a further 5 minutes.

3 Add the tomato purée to the pan and stir into the onion and beetroot mixture. Cover the pan and simmer gently for 10 minutes.

4 Season the mixture with salt and pepper to taste. Transfer to a bowl and leave to cool.

5 To serve, pile the beetroot caviar on to the rye bread and sprinkle with chopped parsley to garnish.

VARIATION
Add 1–2 crushed garlic cloves to the caviar, either cooked with the onion or, if you prefer it, raw, added with the salt and pepper in step 4.

The delicacies of the sea or Russian inland waters, such as caviar, are often a part of the zakuski table, but chopped, flavoured vegetable dishes, known as 'poor man's caviar', are also popular as less expensive alternatives. As with other vegetable caviar, this beetroot caviar is served on rye bread.

Herring Salad Forshmak Seljdj

Serves 6

250g/9oz salted or pickled herring
  fillets
2 eggs
45ml/3 tbsp rapeseed (canola) oil
1 onion, finely chopped
1 hard green apple
40g/1½oz/3 tbsp butter, at
  room temperature
1–2 spring onions (scallions), to
  garnish

1 If using salted herrings, soak the fillets in cold water overnight. The next day, rinse the herring fillets under running water and then drain.

2 Put the eggs in a pan, cover with cold water and bring to the boil. Reduce the heat and simmer for 10 minutes. Meanwhile, heat the oil in a frying pan, add the chopped onion and fry for about 5 minutes, until softened but not browned. Set aside.

3 When the eggs are cooked, drain and put under cold running water. Remove the shell and separate the yolks from the whites.

4 Peel, core and chop the apple and put in a food processor. Add the salted or pickled herring fillets, egg yolks and the butter and process to a paste. Transfer to a bowl and mix in the fried onion.

5 Finely chop the reserved egg whites and finely slice the spring onions. Put the salad on a serving plate and serve garnished with the chopped egg whites and spring onions.

Although the ingredients for this dish are simple, it is usually served at festive occasions. Salted herring fillets must be soaked overnight, so allow time to do this. You can buy ready-made forshmak in Russian delicatessens. It is usually served with ice cold vodka.

Crab Salad Salat iz Krabov

Serves 4–8

1 wedge white cabbage, about
    250g/9oz total weight
250g/9oz can crab meat, preferably
    Russian charka crab meat in its
    own juice
100g/3¾oz/scant ½ cup
    mayonnaise
salt
30ml/2 tbsp finely chopped fresh
    parsley, to garnish
bread slices, to serve

The famous Russian crab meat, charka, is sold in food shops all over the world. The high quality merits the price. However, inventive Russian housewives found a way to supplement the expensive crab meat by adding finely cut, fresh white cabbage. It is surprisingly good.

1 Finely shred the cabbage, discarding the thick stalk. Put in a large bowl and cover with just-boiled water from the kettle.

2 Leave the cabbage to soak for 2–3 minutes. Drain off the water and squeeze the cabbage dry with your hands, transferring the handfuls to a dry bowl as you do so. Set aside and leave to cool.

3 When the cabbage is cool, add the crab meat, in small chunks, and the mayonnaise to the bowl and stir until mixed together. Season with salt to taste and transfer to a serving plate.

4 Garnish the salad with chopped parsley, and serve with bread.

VARIATION
The salad can also be served on pieces of toast, which make a perfect snack to serve with drinks.

Fried Fish with Tartare Sauce
Sudak Olrli s Sousom Tartar

Serves 4

700g/1lb 10oz perch fillet, skinned
   and boned
5ml/1 tsp salt
15ml/1 tbsp fresh lemon juice
115g/4oz/1 cup plain white
   (all-purpose) flour
150ml/¼ pint/⅔ cup light beer
1 egg white
about 1 litre/1¾ pints/4 cups
   rapeseed (canola) oil
lemon wedges, to garnish
green salad, to serve

For the tartare sauce

3 large pickled gherkins
200g/7fl oz/scant 1 cup mayonnaise
15ml/1 tbsp capers
5ml/1 tsp finely chopped fresh dill
15ml/1 tbsp finely chopped fresh
   parsley
2.5ml/½ tsp mustard
1.5ml/¼ tsp salt
1.5ml/¼ tsp ground black pepper

1 To make the tartare sauce, peel and finely chop the gherkins. Put in a bowl with the mayonnaise, capers, dill, parsley and mustard. Mix together. Add salt and pepper to taste, and transfer to a serving bowl.

2 Cut the fish fillets into pieces measuring about 3cm/1¼in and put on a plate. Sprinkle the fish pieces with the salt and lemon juice.

3 Put the flour and beer in a bowl and whisk together until it forms a smooth batter. In a separate bowl, whisk the egg white until it stands in soft peaks then fold into the batter.

4 Heat the oil in a deep fryer to 180°C/350°F or until a cube of bread browns in 1 minute. Dip and turn the fish pieces in the batter and then drop into the hot oil. Fry for 1–2 minutes, until golden. Using a slotted spoon, remove from the pan and drain on kitchen paper.

5 Serve the fish hot with lemon wedges, the tartare sauce and a green salad.

Deep-fried fish – usually perch or pike – served with a tartare sauce is a favourite in Russian restaurants. Here a batter is used, but Russians often use smetana. Serve with a simple green salad for a healthy appetizing meal.

Sole with Vodka Sauce and Caviar Morskoj Jazyk s

1 Season the fish fillets with salt. Roll up and secure each fillet with a cocktail stick (toothpick).

2 Heat the stock in a small pan. Place the fish rolls in the pan, cover and simmer for 5–8 minutes, until the fish is tender. Remove from the pan and keep warm.

3 Meanwhile, make the sauce. Melt the butter in a pan, add the shallots and fry gently for 3–5 minutes, until softened but not browned. Add the flour and stir until well mixed.

4 Gradually add the cream and stock until smooth. Slowly bring to the boil, stirring, until the sauce bubbles. Reduce the heat and simmer for 3–5 minutes, until the sauce thickens. Remove the shallots with a slotted spoon. Add the wine and vodka and bring to the boil. Season with salt and pepper to taste.

5 Pour the sauce over the base of four warmed plates. Place the fish rolls on top and add a spoonful of caviar to each. Garnish with lemon and dill and serve with hot boiled potatoes.

Caviar was once served only with silver spoons to protect the taste. Today, caviar is served on white buttered toast or blinis, or as a luxurious garnish to a delicate fish.

Serves 4

500–600g/1lb 4oz–1lb 6oz sole,
    flounder or plaice fillets
salt
200ml/7fl oz/scant 1 cup fish stock
60ml/4 tbsp caviar
4 lemon wedges and fresh dill, to
    garnish
hot boiled potatoes, to serve

For the vodka sauce

25–40g/1–1½oz/2–3 tbsp butter
5–6 shallots, finely diced
5ml/1 tsp plain white (all-purpose)
    flour
200ml/7fl oz/scant 1 cup double
    (heavy) cream
200ml/7fl oz/scant 1 cup fish stock
100ml/3½fl oz/scant ½ cup dry
    white wine
30ml/2 tbsp vodka
salt and ground black pepper

Fish with Mushroom and Dill Sauce
Sudak s Gribnym Sousom

Serves 4

4 perch fillets, total weight
   500–600g/1lb 4oz–1lb 6oz,
   skinned
5ml/1 tsp salt
plain white (all-purpose) flour, to coat
35–50g/1½–2oz/3–4 tbsp butter
hot boiled new potatoes, to serve

For the dill sauce

2 onions
20 fresh mushrooms
45ml/3 tbsp rapeseed (canola) oil
15ml/1 tbsp plain white
   (all-purpose) flour
200ml/7fl oz/scant 1 cup fish stock
250ml/8fl oz/1 cup double (heavy)
   cream
100ml/3½fl oz/scant ½ cup
   smetana or crème fraîche
1 large bunch fresh dill
100ml/3½fl oz/scant ½ cup dry
   white wine
1–2 dashes mushroom or soy sauce
salt and white pepper

1 To make the sauce, chop the onions and slice the mushrooms. In a large frying pan, heat the oil, add the onions and fry, over a medium high heat, for 3–5 minutes until softened but not browned. Add the sliced mushrooms and fry for a further 5–10 minutes.

2 Meanwhile, season the fish fillets with the salt and coat with the flour. Heat the butter in a large non-stick frying pan over a medium heat. Add the fish and fry for 3 minutes on each side or until golden brown and crisp.

3 Sprinkle the flour into the onions and mushrooms and stir until mixed. Gradually stir in the stock until smooth. Slowly bring to the boil, stirring all the time, until the sauce boils and thickens.

4 Stir the cream and smetana or crème fraîche into the sauce. Reduce the heat and simmer for 3 minutes.

5 Meanwhile, chop the dill. Add the white wine to the sauce and season with the soy sauce, salt and pepper to taste. Stir in the chopped dill.

6 Spoon the sauce over the fish in the pan, reheat gently and serve with hot boiled new potatoes.

VARIATION

Any other firm-fleshed white fish, such as cod or haddock, can be used instead of the perch, and you can substitute frozen or wild mushrooms, such as porcini, for the sauce.

Dill and flat leaf parsley are the herbs most commonly used in Russian cuisine, and both go superbly with many fish dishes. In this recipe the fish is accompanied by a creamy mushroom sauce with a hint of fresh dill.

Beef Stroganoff Bef Stroganov

Serves 4

40–50g/1½–2oz/3–4 tbsp butter
500g/1¼lb beef fillet, very thinly
    sliced
salt and ground black pepper
Salted Cucumbers, diced, to serve

For the sauce

30–45ml/2–3 tbsp rapeseed (canola)
    oil
2–3 onions, thinly sliced
1 chicken stock (bouillon) cube
45ml/3 tbsp tomato purée (paste)
15ml/1 tbsp plain white (all-purpose)
    flour
2–3 bay leaves
4–5 black peppercorns
300ml/½ pint/1¼ cups water
200ml/7fl oz/scant 1 cup double
    (heavy) cream
100ml/3½fl oz/scant ½ cup
    smetana or crème fraîche

For the fried potatoes

90–105ml/6–7 tbsp rapeseed
    (canola) oil
6–8 potatoes, peeled and very thinly
    sliced
salt

1 First make the sauce. Heat the oil in a medium pan. Add the sliced onions and fry over a medium heat for 3–5 minutes. Crumble the stock cube into the onions and fry for a further 1–2 minutes.

2 Add the tomato purée to the pan, then the flour and stir well together. Add the bay leaves and peppercorns and then gradually stir in the water and the cream until smooth. Slowly bring to the boil, stirring all the time, until the sauce boils and thickens. Cover and simmer for 10 minutes. Stir in the smetana or crème fraîche.

3 Meanwhile, fry the potatoes. Heat the oil in a large frying pan. Add the sliced potatoes and fry for 10–15 minutes, turning occasionally. Cover the pan and cook for a further 10–15 minutes, until tender. Season the potatoes with salt to taste.

4 To cook the beef, heat the butter in a frying pan. Add the slices of beef, in batches, and cook quickly, over a high heat, for about 1 minute until browned. Transfer to a plate, season with salt and pepper and keep warm. Repeat with the remaining beef until all the meat is cooked.

5 When you are ready to serve, reheat the sauce, add the beef to the sauce and heat through gently for 2–3 minutes. Serve immediately with the fried potatoes and accompanied with diced Salted Cucumbers.

This famous dish was created at the time of Catherine the Great by Count Alexander Sergeyevich Stroganov. The Count invited poor students into his house, and served this casserole with fried potatoes and Salted Cucumbers.

Little Beef Dumplings Peljmeni

1 First make the pastry. Put the eggs, water, oil, salt and half of the flour in a food processor and process until well blended. Add the remaining flour, in batches, to form a smooth pastry. Turn the pastry on to a lightly floured surface and knead for 5 minutes. Put in a plastic bag and leave to rest for 30 minutes, or overnight, in a cold place.

2 To make the filling, finely grate the onion and put in a bowl. Add the minced beef and pork, salt and pepper and mix together. Set aside.

3 To make the dumplings, cut the pastry into eight pieces. Work with one piece at a time, keeping the remaining pieces in the plastic bag to prevent them from drying out. On a floured surface, roll the piece of pastry into a roll, the thickness of a finger. Cut the roll into 10–12 small pieces.

4 Flatten out each piece to a round, about 3cm/1¼ in in diameter, and then roll out into a thinner round, 5–6cm/2–2½in in diameter. Spread each round with 5m/1 tsp of the meat mixture, leaving a small uncovered edge. Fold and pinch together the rounds to form a half-moon shape.

5 As you make the dumplings, put them on a floured baking sheet. When the sheet is full, put it in the freezer. When frozen, transfer the dumplings to a plastic bag and keep frozen until required.

6 When you are ready to serve the dumplings, take the amount you need from the freezer and put in a pan of lightly salted boiling water. Simmer until the dumplings float to the surface then simmer for a further 1 minute. Using a slotted spoon, scoop out of the water and serve immediately, sprinkled with vinegar, melted butter, salt and pepper. A small amount of the cooking water and smetana may also be added to taste, if wished.

These tiny Siberian dumplings are traditionally accompanied by red wine vinegar, melted butter, and ground black pepper. Russians expect to eat about 40 pelmeni at a time.

Makes 80–100
For the pastry
2 eggs
150ml/¼ pint/⅔ cup water
15ml/1 tbsp rapeseed (canola) oil
2.5ml/½ tsp salt
360g/12½oz/3⅛ cups plain white
    (all-purpose) flour, plus extra for
    dusting

For the filling
1 onion, total weight 100g/3¾oz
200g/7oz minced (ground) beef
200g/7oz minced (ground) pork
7.5ml/1½ tsp salt
2–2.5ml/⅓–½ tsp ground black
    pepper
red wine vinegar, melted butter, salt
    and ground black pepper, and
    smetana (optional), to serve

Rabbit in Smetana
Krolik v Smetane

1 Cut the rabbit meat into bitesize chunks. Heat the butter in a large frying pan until melted and beginning to turn brown. Add the rabbit pieces and fry over a medium heat, stirring occasionally, for 10 minutes, until browned on all sides. Season the rabbit with salt and pepper.

2 Add the shallots and water and half the beef stock to the pan, cover and cook over a low heat for 1–1½ hours, until the meat is tender. If necessary, add a little additional water.

3 Put the rest of the beef stock, the smetana or crème fraîche and the chopped parsley in a jug (pitcher) and mix together well. Add the mixture to the meat, bring to the boil then reduce the heat and simmer for 10–15 minutes.

4 To serve, put the meat on to a warmed serving dish and spoon over the sauce. Garnish the rabbit with parsley sprigs and accompany with boiled potatoes, rice or pasta.

COOK'S TIP
If you have difficulty in buying rabbit from a supermarket, you can order it from a butcher or often find it at a food market. Chicken can be used instead.

Serves 4–6

1 rabbit, total weight about
　1.5kg/3¼lb, cleaned and skinned
40g/1½oz/3 tbsp butter
salt and ground black pepper
12 shallots
45–60ml/3–4 tbsp water
200ml/7fl oz/scant 1 cup beef stock
300ml/½ pint/1¼ cups smetana or
　crème fraîche
15g/½oz/¼ cup finely chopped fresh
　parsley, plus 4–5 sprigs, to
　garnish
boiled potatoes, rice or pasta, to
　serve

Smetana, a sour cream, is an ingredient in many Russian dishes. Rabbit cooked in a sauce of smetana acquires a delicate, mild flavour. Boiled potatoes are the traditional accompaniment.

Venison Ragoût
Ragu iz Oleniny

1 Cut the meat into chunky pieces. Chop the onions, dice the turnips and crush the juniper berries. Heat the butter and oil in a flameproof casserole. Add the meat and fry, stirring frequently, for about 10 minutes, until browned on all sides.

2 Add the onions to the pan and fry for 3–5 minutes. Add the turnips and fry, stirring all the time, for a further 5 minutes. Crumble in the stock cube and add the tomato purée.

3 Sprinkle the flour over the meat and fry, stirring all the time, for 1 minute. Add the crushed juniper berries, bay leaves, peppercorns and gradually stir in the water. Bring to the boil then reduce the heat, cover and simmer for about 1½ hours, until the meat is tender.

4 Stir the cream into the pan and cook for a further 10 minutes. Season the ragoût with salt and pepper to taste and serve hot with boiled or mashed potatoes.

VARIATION
If you use bear fillet, increase the cooking time by about 1½ hours.

Serves 4
600g/1lb 6oz venison or elk fillet
2 onions
500g/1¼lb turnips
5–6 juniper berries
40g/1¼oz/3 tbsp butter
30ml/2 tbsp rapeseed (canola) oil
1 beef stock (bouillon) cube
60–75ml/4–5 tbsp tomato purée
    (paste)
15ml/1 tbsp plain white (all-purpose)
    flour
2–3 bay leaves
4–5 black peppercorns
500ml/17fl oz/generous 2 cups
    water
300ml/½ pint/1¼ cups double
    (heavy) cream
salt and ground black pepper
mashed or boiled potatoes, to serve

Bear meat was originally used in this recipe, which dates from the times when bear was hunted in Russia, but venison or elk fillet can be substituted.

Chicken Kiev Kotlety pa Kievski s

1 On the underside of the chicken breast fillets, separate the small finger-thick fillets from the larger fillets. Put one fillet at a time on a sheet of oiled clear film (plastic wrap). Cover with another sheet of clear film and beat with a wooden rolling pin until the large fillets are 5mm/¼in thick and the smaller fillets 3mm/⅛in thick. When flat, remove from the clear film and put on a board.

2 Cut the butter into four sticks. Put the white pepper, garlic powder and 1.5ml/¼ tsp salt on a plate and mix together. Roll the butter sticks in the mixture and place one stick in the centre of each large fillet. Cover with a small flattened fillet and fold the edges of the large fillet up and around to form a tight parcel that holds together. If necessary, secure each parcel with a cocktail stick (toothpick). Sprinkle the parcels with salt. Chill until ready to cook.

3 To make the mushroom sauce, chop the mushrooms. Put in a pan and cook over a medium heat, stirring frequently, until most of the liquid has absorbed. Turn up the heat, add the butter and stir-fry the mushrooms for 5–10 minutes. Sprinkle the flour into the mushrooms and stir until mixed. Gradually stir in the cream, a little at a time, until smooth. Slowly bring to the boil, stirring, until the sauce boils. Reduce the heat and simmer for 10 minutes. Season to taste.

4 Meanwhile, preheat the oven to 220°C/425°F/Gas 7. Line a baking sheet with foil. Spread the breadcrumbs on a plate. Lightly beat the eggs in a small bowl. Brush the chicken parcels with the beaten eggs then roll in the breadcrumbs to coat on all sides. Brush again with the beaten eggs and roll again in the breadcrumbs until evenly coated.

5 Heat the oil in a deep fryer until a cube of bread browns in 1 minute. Add the chicken parcels to the hot oil and deep-fry for 3–4 minutes, until golden brown. Remove from the pan and place on the prepared baking sheet. Fold in the foil to cover. Bake in the oven for 5–10 minutes. Serve with cooked rice, sugarsnap peas and the mushroom sauce.

Serves 4

4 skinless chicken breast fillets
65g/2½oz/5 tbsp cold butter
1.5ml/¼ tsp ground white pepper
2.5ml/½ tsp garlic powder
salt
150g/5oz/3 cups fresh white
    breadcrumbs
2–3 eggs
750ml/1¼ pints/3 cups rapeseed
    (canola) oil
cooked rice and sugarsnap peas, to
    serve

For the mushroom sauce

250g/9oz fresh porcini
25g/1oz/2 tbsp butter
15ml/1 tbsp plain white
    (all-purpose) flour
300ml/½ pint/1¼ cups whipping
    cream
salt and ground black pepper

These classic Ukrainian chicken breasts are often served with mushroom sauce. Traditionally the sauce is served in little pastry shells, called croustades, placed on individual serving plates.

Cheese Dumplings Lenivye Vareniki

Serves 4

500g/1¼lb/2½ cups ricotta cheese
    or cottage cheese
2 eggs
salt
200g/7oz/1¾ cups plain white
    (all-purpose) flour
25g/1oz/2 tbsp butter
smetana or crème fraîche, to serve

1 Put the cheese, eggs and a pinch of salt in a bowl and mix well together. Add the flour and fold in until it is thoroughly combined. The dough should be soft and form into a ball. Remove the ball from the bowl and put on a floured surface or board.

2 Cut the dough into eight equal pieces and roll each piece into a sausage shape about as thick as a finger. Cut each sausage into 2cm/¾in sections.

3 Bring a large pan of water to the boil and add 5ml/1 tsp salt. Put half of the dumplings in the pan and simmer for 2 minutes, until they float to the surface. Using a slotted spoon, remove the dumplings from the pan, transfer to a colander and put under cold running water for a few seconds. Repeat with the second batch of dumplings in the same way.

4 Heat the butter in a large pan. Add the drained dumplings and sauté them until thoroughly warmed through and slightly golden. Serve immediately with a bowl of smetana or crème fraîche.

COOK'S TIPS

When the dumplings have been boiled, it is important to rinse them under cold running water straight away for a couple of seconds. This is partly to stop them cooking, and also to rinse off some of the starch and stop them from sticking together. Serve these dumplings with fried bacon for non-vegetarians, or as a dessert with smetana and sugar.

Cottage cheese, Italian ricotta, or another fresh soft cheese combines well in these delicate but simple Russian dumplings, which are very similar to Italian gnocchi.

Puff Pastry Cabbage Pie
Pirog Sloenyj s Kapustoj

1 Discard the outer leaves and hard stalk of the cabbage, cut in half and chop finely. Heat the butter in a medium frying pan over a low heat, add the cabbage and stir-fry for 25 minutes until softened; don't allow it to brown. Season and leave to cool.

2 Put the eggs in a pan, cover with cold water and bring to the boil. Reduce the heat, and simmer for 10 minutes, then drain and put under cold running water. Remove the shells from the eggs then chop and put in a large bowl. Add the cabbage to the bowl and mix.

3 Preheat the oven to 220°C/425°F/ Gas 7. Put the sheet of pastry on a dampened baking tray. Spread the cabbage and egg mixture lengthways on one half of the pastry sheet. Brush the edges with water and fold the other side over to enclose. Seal together by pressing with a fork along the join. It should look like a tightly packed loaf.

4 To make the glaze, whisk together the egg yolk and water. Brush the pastry with the mixture and make some small holes in the top with a fork. Sprinkle the top of the pastry with the breadcrumbs.

5 Bake the pie in the oven for 12–15 minutes, until the pastry is crisp and golden brown. Leave the baked pie to rest for 5–10 minutes then cut into portions and serve.

COOK'S TIP
This pie is made with one large sheet of ready-made puff pastry, which can be bought chilled in one roll. The size should be about 40 x 20cm/16 x 8in. However, if your sheets are smaller, it is possible to put three smaller sheets together and seal them into one large one.

Serves 4–6
300–400g/11–14oz cabbage
40–50g/1½–2oz/3–4 tbsp butter
3 eggs
1 sheet ready-made chilled puff
    pastry, measuring about 40 x
    20cm/16 x 8in
salt

For the glaze
1 egg yolk
5ml/1 tsp water
15ml/1 tbsp fresh white
    breadcrumbs

Crisp puff pastry with a very soft cabbage filling is a favourite dish for Russians to eat on a Saturday night when the whole family is gathered around the table.

Vegetable Ragoût
Ragu iz Ovocshej

Serves 4
3–4 carrots
1 swede (rutabaga)
1 turnip
1 parsnip
10ml/2 tsp sunflower oil
1 large onion, finely chopped
100–200ml/3½–7fl oz/scant ½–1
  cup vegetable stock or lightly
  salted water
105ml/7 tbsp finely chopped fresh
  parsley
15g/½oz/1 tbsp butter
dark rye bread and butter, to serve

1 Cut the carrots, swede, turnip and parsnip into small chunks. Heat the oil in a flameproof casserole, add the chopped onion and fry over a medium heat, for 3–5 minutes until softened.

2 Add the carrots, swede, turnip and parsnip to the pan and fry, stirring frequently, for a further 10 minutes. Add the stock and bring to the boil. Cover with a lid and simmer for 20 minutes until the vegetables are soft.

3 Add the chopped parsley and the butter to the pan and stir until the butter has melted. Season with salt to taste and serve hot.

VARIATION
Add 100g/3¾oz/scant 1 cup fresh or frozen peas to the ragoût 3 minutes before adding the chopped fresh parsley and butter.

Russians prefer to eat their vegetables very soft and very hot. Both are illustrated in this recipe. Serve the ragoût with dark rye bread and a little butter.

Sauerkraut Salad with Cranberries
Salat iz Kisloj Kapusty s Kljukvoj

Serves 4–6

500g/1¼lb sauerkraut
2 red apples
100–200g/3¾–7oz/scant 1–1¾
    cups fresh cranberries or
    lingonberries
30ml/2 tbsp sugar
60–75ml/4–5 tbsp sunflower oil
2–3 sprigs fresh parsley, to garnish

Cabbage is a staple ingredient in Russia and the best soured cabbage can be bought in the market halls, where you are invited to taste both the cabbage and the brine. It is not unusual for a customer to taste up to ten different kinds of cabbage before making a decision.

1 Put the sauerkraut in a colander and drain thoroughly. Taste, and if you find it is too sour, rinse it under cold running water then drain well.

2 Put the sauerkraut in a large bowl. Slice or cut the apples into slices or wedges. Add the apples and the cranberries or lingonberries to the sauerkraut. Sprinkle over the sugar, pour the oil on top and mix all the ingredients well together.

3 To serve, turn the sauerkraut into a serving bowl and garnish with the parsley sprigs.

Potato Cakes with Mushroom Sauce
Kartofeljnye Korlety s Gribnym Sousom

Serves 4

1kg/2¼lb floury potatoes
salt
50g/2oz/¼ cup butter
100ml/3½fl oz/scant ½ cup warm milk
1 egg
75g/3oz/1½ cups fresh white breadcrumbs
15ml/1 tbsp rapeseed (canola) oil
1 quantity of Mushroom Sauce (see page 45) to serve

1 Peel and cut the potatoes into even pieces. Put in a pan of salted water, bring to the boil then reduce the heat and simmer for 20 minutes, until soft. Drain, return to the pan and mash until smooth.

2 Add 15g/½oz/1 tbsp of the butter and the milk to the potatoes and mix together until smooth. Leave to cool, then add the egg and mix together. Season the potatoes with salt to taste.

3 Wet your hands under cold water, take a handful of the mashed potato and form into a cake. Repeat with the remaining mashed potato to make eight cakes. Spread the breadcrumbs on a plate and turn the cakes in the breadcrumbs to coat on both sides. Set aside.

4 To cook the potato cakes, heat the remaining 40g/1½oz/3 tbsp butter and the oil in a large frying pan, add the cakes and fry over a medium heat, for about 3–5 minutes on each side, turning once, until they are golden brown.

5 Gently warm the Mushroom Sauce, and serve the potato cakes hot, accompanied by the sauce.

Potatoes are the perfect accompaniment to many Russian dishes and are served fried, boiled, mashed and in gratins, with fish, meat or vegetables. Russians believe potatoes and mushrooms make the perfect combination, and those who do not pick their own mushrooms will dry bought ones at home and thread them on a string.

Baked Cheesecake
Zapekanka iz Tvoroga

1 Preheat the oven to 180°C/350°F/Gas 4. Use the butter to grease the bottom and sides of a 20cm/8in loose-bottomed cake tin (pan) then pour in the breadcrumbs and tip and shake until the insides of the tin are well coated with the breadcrumbs.

2 Separate the egg yolks from the egg whites into two separate large bowls. Finely chop the candied peel and add to the egg yolks. Add the cottage or ricotta cheese, sugar, raisins, lemon rind and semolina and mix well together.

3 Whisk the egg whites until they are stiff and hold their shape then fold into the cheese mixture. Spoon the mixture into the prepared tin.

4 Bake the cake in the oven for 30–40 minutes, until a skewer, inserted in the centre, comes out dry. Leave the cake to cool in the tin.

5 Slide a knife around the edge of the cake and carefully remove it from the tin. Place on a serving plate and dust with sifted icing sugar.

6 Serve the cheesecake with smetana or crème fraîche or whipped cream and fresh berries.

Serves 6–8

15g/½oz/1 tbsp butter
45ml/3 tbsp fresh white
    breadcrumbs
4 eggs
100g/3¾oz mixed (candied) peel
500g/1¼lb/2 cups cottage or ricotta
    cheese
90g/3½oz/½ cup caster (superfine)
    sugar
50g/2oz/scant ½ cup raisins
grated rind (zest) of 1 lemon
45ml/3 tbsp semolina
icing (confectioners') sugar, for
    dusting
smetana, crème fraîche or whipped
    cream, and fresh berries, such as
    strawberries, raspberries,
    blueberries or redcurrants, to
    serve

Russians love their tea, and tea drinking is an ancient Russian tradition. It is popular to have parties where nothing but tea and sweet accompaniments are served. These include cherry jam, gooseberry jam and whole strawberry jam (put in the tea or eaten from special small plates), chocolates, fudge and soft spicy ginger cookies. The highlight of the tea is a cheesecake, flavoured with raisins, preserved peel and lemon.

Small Blueberry Pies Vatrushki s Chernikoj

1 To make the dough, melt the butter in a small pan. Add the milk, water, salt and sugar and heat until warm to the finger. Pour the mixture into a large bowl. Add the egg and mix together.

2 Put the flour and yeast in a bowl and mix together. Stir in the butter mixture, a little at a time, until combined. Knead the dough in the bowl for at least 5 minutes. Cover the bowl with a dish towel and leave the dough to rise in a warm place for 30 minutes until it has doubled in size.

3 Turn the dough on to a lightly floured surface. Cut the dough into 24 pieces and form each piece into a ball. Leave to rest for 5–10 minutes.

4 Meanwhile, prepare the filling. Put the blueberries in a bowl, add the sugar and potato flour and mix together.

5 Preheat the oven to 200°C/400°F/Gas 6. Grease a large baking tray. Flatten each ball to a round measuring about 15cm/6in in diameter.

6 Place the rounds on the baking tray. Place 45ml/3 tbsp of the blueberry mixture in the centre of each round then fold a small edge up around the mixture. Bake the pies for 10–15 minutes, until golden brown.

7 Meanwhile, make the glaze. Put the smetana or crème fraîche and the sugar in a bowl and mix together.

8 When the pies are baked, gently spoon a little of the glaze over each pie. Dust the tops with sifted icing sugar. Serve hot or cold.

Delicious little blueberry pies are perfect as a dessert after Sunday lunch. Alternatively, serve them in the afternoon; seat your guests in the garden and bring out the samovar. Serve these home-made temptations on a Russian tray decorated with beautiful fresh flowers, with lots of hot tea.

Makes 10

For the dough
50g/2oz/¼ cup butter
200ml/7fl oz/scant 1 cup milk
45ml/3 tbsp water
2.5ml/½ tsp salt
7.5ml/1½ tsp caster (superfine) sugar
1 small (US medium) egg
400g/14oz/3½ cups plain white (all-purpose) flour
large pinch of easy-blend (rapid-rise) dried yeast

For the filling
300–350g/11–12oz/2¾–3 cups blueberries, fresh or frozen
25g/1oz/2 tbsp caster (superfine) sugar
15ml/1 tbsp potato flour

For the glaze
150ml/¼ pint/⅔ cup smetana or crème fraîche
45ml/3 tbsp caster (superfine) sugar
icing (confectioners') sugar, for dusting

Pashka Pashka

Serves 6–8

500g/1¼lb/2½ cups ricotta cheese
  or cottage cheese
75g/3oz/6 tbsp unsalted butter,
  softened
275g/10oz/1½ cups caster
  (superfine) sugar
30ml/2 tbsp vanilla sugar
150ml/¼ pint/⅔ cup whipping cream
30ml/2 tbsp smetana or crème
  fraîche
2 egg yolks
40g/1½oz/generous ¼ cup raisins
grated rind (zest) 1 lemon
glacé (candied) orange or lemon and
  blanched almonds, to decorate

1 If using cottage cheese, push the cheese through a sieve (strainer). Put the ricotta or cottage cheese in a sieve and stand the sieve over a bowl. Leave to drain overnight in a cold place.

2 Line a clean 750ml/1¼ pints/3 cups coffee filter, or a flower pot with a drainage hole, with damp muslin (cheesecloth) allowing the edges of the muslin to overhang the edges. Transfer the drained cheese into a bowl, add the butter, sugar and vanilla sugar and beat together until smooth.

3 Pour the whipping cream into a separate bowl and whisk until it forms soft peaks. Stir the cream, smetana or crème fraîche and egg yolks into the cheese mixture then whisk until fluffy and smooth. Add the raisins and grated lemon rind and stir together.

4 Spoon the mixture into the lined holder and fold the edges of the muslin into the centre. Cover with a small saucer that fits inside the holder and put a 500g/1¼lb weight on top. Stand in a bowl or soup plate and leave in a cold place, to drain, for one to three days.

5 Remove the weight and saucer. Unfold the muslin and very carefully turn the paskha out on to a serving plate. Remove the muslin. Serve the Paskha decorated with candied fruits and nuts.

This fresh cheese and dried fruit dessert is made by mixing the ingredients together, putting them in a lined mould and letting all the liquid drain away, creating a firm, dome-shaped pudding. The usual shape is a pyramid, made in a wooden mould, but a coffee filter-holder or a clean plastic flower pot work well. Paskha needs to be made a few days in advance, and is traditionally eaten to celebrate the end of Lent.

Serves 8–10
200ml/7fl oz/scant 1 cup milk
350–425g/12–15oz/3–3⅔ cups
   plain white (all-purpose) flour
185g/6½oz/scant 1 cup caster
   (superfine) sugar
large pinch easy-blend (rapid-rise)
   dried yeast
115g/4oz/½ cup butter, plus extra
   for greasing
15ml/1 tbsp vanilla sugar
2.5ml/½ tsp salt
5ml/1 tsp ground cardamom
3 egg yolks
150g/5oz/1 cup raisins

Russian Easter Cake Kulitj

1 Pour the milk into a small pan and heat until warm to the finger. Remove from the heat. Put 325g/11½oz/scant 3 cups of the flour, half of the sugar and the yeast in a food processor and mix together.

2 Add the warm milk to the processor and mix until combined. Cover and leave to rise in a warm place for about 30 minutes, until doubled in size.

3 Melt the butter. Add the remaining sugar, the vanilla sugar, salt, cardamom and melted butter, reserving 15ml/1 tbsp, to the risen dough and mix together until smooth. Add the egg yolks, one at a time, until combined.

4 Generously grease a 17cm/6½in round, 10cm/4in deep, cake tin (pan) or 1.5 litre/2½ pint/6¼ cup soufflé dish with butter.

5 Transfer the dough to a lightly floured surface and knead in the remaining flour and the raisins. Put the dough into the prepared tin or dish, cover and leave to rise for 30 minutes.

6 Preheat the oven to 180°C/350°F/Gas 4. Brush the dough with half of the reserved melted butter. Bake in the oven for 30 minutes. Brush with the remaining melted butter and bake for a further 20–30 minutes, until risen and golden brown. Remove from the tin or dish and transfer to a wire rack to cool.

A traditional Easter dinner in Russia always starts with zakuski and ends with a home-made kulitj, a high, round cake flavoured with cardamom and vanilla. Kulitj is also served at Easter and between kulitj and paskha one feasts on Easter eggs. Traditionally, the kulitj, pashka and Easter eggs are blessed by the priests.

Crêpes with a Cheese Filling
Blinchiki s Tvorogom

Serves 4
50g/2oz/¼ cup butter
3 eggs
2.5ml/½ tsp salt
2ml/⅓ tsp caster (superfine) sugar
200ml/7fl oz/scant 1 cup warm
    water
185g/6½oz/1⅔ cups plain white
    (all-purpose) flour
350ml/12fl oz/1½ cups milk
60–75ml/4–5 tbsp rapeseed (canola)
    oil, for brushing, and 30–45ml/
    2–3 tbsp, for frying
crème fraîche, and caster (superfine)
    sugar, to serve

For the filling
500g/1¼lb/2½ cups ricotta cheese,
2 egg yolks
30–45ml/2–3 tbsp caster (superfine)
    sugar

Fresh cheese is an everyday food in Russia and is often eaten on its own. By omitting the sugar, these crêpes can be adapted to a savoury dish.

1 Melt the butter. Whisk the eggs, salt and sugar together in a bowl. Add the water, then gradually whisk in the flour. Stir in the milk, a little at a time, with the melted butter.

2 Heat a non-stick frying pan over a medium heat. Brush it with a little oil and pour in a thin layer of batter. As soon as the surface has set, turn the crêpe over and cook the other side. Fry the remaining crêpes in the same way, brushing the pan with oil each time and stacking when cooked.

3 To make the filling, put the ricotta cheese and egg yolks in a bowl and mix together. Add sugar to taste. Place 45ml/3 tbsp of the filling in the centre of each crêpe and fold over to create an envelope.

4 Heat the oil in a frying pan. Add the envelopes, joint-side down, and fry, over a medium heat, for 1–2 minutes. Turn and fry the other sides for 1–2 minutes, until golden brown. Serve the pancakes with crème fraîche and sugar for sprinkling.

Nutritional notes

Beetroot Soup: Energy 127kcal/535kJ; Protein 4g; Carbohydrate 20.2g, of which sugars 17.7g; Fat 4g, of which saturates 2.3g; Cholesterol 9mg; Calcium 60mg; Fibre 5g; Sodium 143mg.

Fresh Cabbage Soup: Energy 273kcal/1141kJ; Protein 6g; Carbohydrate 36.7g, of which sugars 17.4g; Fat 12.2g, of which saturates 5.8g; Cholesterol 21mg; Calcium 122mg; Fibre 7.2g; Sodium 106mg.

Cold Kvass Soup: Energy 353kcal/1473kJ; Protein 27.6g; Carbohydrate 17.6g, of which sugars 17.3g; Fat 19.8g, of which saturates 10.3g; Cholesterol 169mg; Calcium 363mg; Fibre 0.8g; Sodium 305mg.

Russian Pancakes: Energy 89kcal/372kJ; Protein 2g; Carbohydrate 7.6g, of which sugars 0.7g; Fat 5.9g, of which saturates 0.9g; Cholesterol 21mg; Calcium 30mg; Fibre 0.3g; Sodium 16mg.

Chopped Herring Salad: Energy 212kcal/875kJ; Protein 7.6g; Carbohydrate 3.2g, of which sugars 2.8g; Fat 18.9g, of which saturates 4.6g; Cholesterol 97mg; Calcium 32mg; Fibre 0.3g; Sodium 223mg.

Crab Salad: Energy 121kcal/501kJ; Protein 6.4g; Carbohydrate 1.9g, of which sugars 1.8g; Fat 9.8g, of which saturates 1.5g; Cholesterol 32mg; Calcium 66mg; Fibre 1g; Sodium 232mg.

Salted cucumbers: Energy 503kcal/2086kJ; Protein 8.8g; Carbohydrate 62.7g, of which sugars 61.6g; Fat 25.1g, of which saturates 16.3g; Cholesterol 68mg; Calcium 238mg; Fibre 6.5g; Sodium 80mg.

Beetroot Caviar: Energy 60kcal/251kJ; Protein 1.1g; Carbohydrate 4.9g, of which sugars 4.2g; Fat 4.2g, of which saturates 0.5g; Cholesterol 0mg; Calcium 14mg; Fibre 1.1g; Sodium 34mg.

Fried Fish with Tartare Sauce: Energy 719kcal/2986kJ; Protein 36.7g; Carbohydrate 24.3g, of which sugars 2.1g; Fat 53.4g, of which saturates 7.6g; Cholesterol 118mg; Calcium 95mg; Fibre 1.8g; Sodium 352mg.

Sole with Vodka Sauce and Caviar: Energy 470kcal/1952kJ; Protein 27.9g; Carbohydrate 3.2g, of which sugars 1.9g; Fat 35g, of which saturates

20.4g; Cholesterol 188mg; Calcium 103mg; Fibre 0.3g; Sodium 548mg.

Fish with Mushroom and Dill Sauce: Energy 706kcal/2924kJ; Protein 31.2g; Carbohydrate 15.6g, of which sugars 7.5g; Fat 56.3g, of which saturates 30.7g; Cholesterol 191mg; Calcium 98mg; Fibre 1.8g; Sodium 137mg.

Beef Stroganoff: Energy 919kcal/3810kJ; Protein 32.5g; Carbohydrate 36g, of which sugars 11.7g; Fat 72.6g, of which saturates 34.6g; Cholesterol 194mg; Calcium 94mg; Fibre 3.4g; Sodium 177mg.

Little Beef Dumplings: Energy 381kcal/1605kJ; Protein 20.9g; Carbohydrate 47.9g, of which sugars 1.8g; Fat 13.1g, of which saturates 4.4g; Cholesterol 105mg; Calcium 103mg; Fibre 2.1g; Sodium 74mg.

Rabbit in Smetana: Energy 436kcal/1809kJ; Protein 33.9g; Carbohydrate 6.7g, of which sugars 5g; Fat 30.5g, of which saturates 19.5g; Cholesterol 193mg; Calcium 121mg; Fibre 1.4g; Sodium 129mg.

Venison Ragoût: Energy 758kcal/3148kJ; Protein 37.6g; Carbohydrate 19.1g, of which sugars 13.7g; Fat 60.7g, of which saturates 32.4g; Cholesterol 199mg; Calcium 139mg; Fibre 4.7g; Sodium 200mg.

Chicken Kiev: Energy 938kcal/3901kJ; Protein 46.2g; Carbohydrate 31.5g, of which sugars 3.3g; Fat 70.7g, of which saturates 33.9g; Cholesterol 327mg; Calcium 122mg; Fibre 1.5g; Sodium 568mg.

Cheese Dumplings: Energy 803kcal/3328kJ; Protein 11.8g; Carbohydrate 38.9g, of which sugars 0.8g; Fat 68g, of which saturates 41.3g; Cholesterol 227mg;

Calcium 208mg; Fibre 1.6g; Sodium 450mg.

Puff Pastry Cabbage Pie: Energy 333kcal/1388kJ; Protein 7.9g; Carbohydrate 25.3g, of which sugars 3.3g; Fat 23.6g, of which saturates 4.5g; Cholesterol 143mg; Calcium 80mg; Fibre 1.2g; Sodium 276mg.

Vegetable Ragoût: Energy 122kcal/506kJ; Protein 2.6g; Carbohydrate 15.9g, of which sugars 13.3g; Fat 5.7g, of which saturates 2.3g; Cholesterol 8mg; Calcium 137mg; Fibre 6.3g; Sodium 68mg.

Sauerkraut Salad with Cranberries: Energy 105kcal/437kJ; Protein 1.3g; Carbohydrate 8.8g, of which sugars 8.8g; Fat 7.4g, of which saturates 0.9g; Cholesterol 0mg; Calcium 49mg; Fibre 3.1g; Sodium 493mg.

Potato Cakes with Mushroom Sauce: Energy 389kcal/1637kJ; Protein 8.9g; Carbohydrate 56g, of which sugars 5g; Fat 16g, of which saturates 7.7g; Cholesterol 76mg; Calcium 79mg; Fibre 2.9g; Sodium 274mg.

Baked Cheesecake: Energy 297kcal/1239kJ; Protein 7.6g; Carbohydrate 27.2g, of which sugars 19g; Fat 18g, of which saturates 9g; Cholesterol 83mg; Calcium 56mg; Fibre 1.1g; Sodium 139mg.

Small Blueberry Pies: Energy 371kcal/1559kJ; Protein 4.4g; Carbohydrate 55.8g, of which sugars 25.7g; Fat 16g, of which saturates 4.9g; Cholesterol 8mg; Calcium 93mg; Fibre 3.2g; Sodium 228mg.

Pashka: Energy 369kcal/1544kJ; Protein 9.3g; Carbohydrate 41.9g, of which sugars 41.9g; Fat 19.1g, of which saturates 11.5g; Cholesterol 100mg; Calcium 118mg; Fibre 0.1g; Sodium 256mg.

Russian Easter Cake: Energy 346kcal/1459kJ; Protein 5.3g; Carbohydrate 57.9g, of which sugars 31.3g; Fat 12g, of which saturates 6.7g; Cholesterol 86mg; Calcium 99mg; Fibre 1.4g; Sodium 92mg.

Crêpes with a Cheese Filling: Energy 1054kcal/4371kJ; Protein 17.5g; Carbohydrate 48g, of which sugars 12.7g; Fat 89.6g, of which saturates 47.9g; Cholesterol 394mg; Calcium 332mg; Fibre 1.4g; Sodium 547mg.

Index